Railways & Recollections 1979

Contents

First published in 2012

British Library Cataloguing in Publication Data

A catalogue record for this book is available from the British Library.

ISBN 978 1 85794 415 0

Silver Link Publishing Ltd
The Trundle
Ringstead Road
Great Addington
Kettering
Northants NN14 4BW

Tel/Fax: 01536 330588

email: sales@nostalgiacollection.com
Website: www.nostalgiacollection.com

Printed and bound in the Czech Republic

Frontispiece: **PENISTONE** Two Class 76 locomotives built for the 1,500V DC electrification between Manchester and Sheffield/Wath have just worked a heavy freight train bound for Immingham via the Woodhead route on Thursday 17 May 1979. Time was running out for this system, and the route between Penistone and Hadfield was closed in 1981.

Right: **KENSINGTON GARDENS** This replica of *Rocket*, the locomotive that had won the famous Rainhill Trials 150 years earlier, ran on a specially laid track in London during the summer of 1979, and was photographed near the Albert Hall on Wednesday 29 August.

Introduction: Now is the winter of our discontent...

'Now is the winter of our discontent…' began Richard, Duke of Gloucester, in Act 1, Scene 1 of *Richard III* by William Shakespeare. Well over 350 years later, the phrase 'winter of discontent' was used to describe the opening months of 1979. In November 1978 Ford had agreed to give its workforce a pay rise of 17% in order to resolve an industrial dispute – an offer way above the Government guideline maximum of 5%. The resultant discrediting of the Government's pay restraint target soon led to an outbreak of strikes that in total added up to the biggest labour stoppage in Britain since the General Strike of 1926.

Early January 1979 saw the TGWU call the lorry drivers out on strike. A series of strikes, some official, some unofficial, soon spread across the country; ambulance crews, hospital cleaners, railway staff, refuse collectors, school caretakers, civil servants and in some areas even grave-diggers came out on strike. To compound the problems caused by the strike, both January and February were exceptionally cold with snowfalls occurring in many parts of the country. On 14 February what became known as the Valentine's Day Concordat between the Government and the TUC paved the way for the ending of the 'winter of discontent' by largely conceding to the demands of the strikers, although some stoppages continued into March.

On 28 March the Government lost a vote of confidence in the House of Commons by one vote, and the following day the Prime Minister, James Callaghan, announced that a General Election would take place on 3 May. When the election results had been counted, the Conservative Party had gained 339 seats, giving the new Prime Minister, Margaret Thatcher, a majority of 43; this was on a turnout of 76% and the Conservative share of the total vote was only 44%.

During the summer the Government made a start on tax cuts and public spending cuts, but industrial relations problems soon reared their head again. A strike by television technicians started on 10 August, and shut down the whole of the ITV network until 23 October (in 1979 the UK television network consisted of just three channels, BBC1, BBC2 and ITV). However, in November *The Times* newspaper was published for the first time in almost a year after a dispute between management and the unions over new technology and manning levels was finally settled. Just before Christmas the Government published a Housing Bill that would give council tenants the right to buy their homes, starting from the following year. The average price of a house in Britain in 1979 was £13,650.

On the railways, 1979 saw the launch of the Family Railcard, which in its original form allowed one adult paying the normal full or day return fare to be accompanied by a second adult and up to four children at fares of 50p each. A particularly encouraging development in Scotland during October was the inauguration of the Argyle line, linking the previously separate systems north and south of the Clyde; this greatly improved local access to central Glasgow, and the recast services also achieved better utilisation of rolling stock. There was also a general programme of refurbishing the Southern Region's 4-CEP and 4-BEP units, which dated from the late 1950s/early 1960s, for further service; the restyled units certainly looked more modern inside, but some of us considered that they were more roomy and comfortable as they were first built.

On the London Underground system, the Prince of Wales opened the first section of the Jubilee Line on 30 April. This included what had previously been the Stanmore branch of the Bakerloo Line plus 2.75 miles of new line from Baker Street to Charing Cross with intermediate stations at Bond Street and Green Park; passenger services began on 1 May. The original plan had been to extend the line from Charing Cross onwards to Aldwych and Cannon Street in due course, but in the event the line was extended from Green Park via Westminster, Waterloo, London Bridge and West Ham to Stratford, with the spur to the 1979 terminus at Charing Cross being closed in November 1999.

Let us now look back at the eventful year that brought to a close what had in many ways been an unusual decade. Let us look back to 1979…

Chris Harris
Poole, Dorset

June 2012

Look North

LEEDS Looking resplendent in British Rail 'Inter-City 125' branding, High Speed Train (HST) unit No 254030 was virtually new and in showroom condition when photographed at Leeds on Saturday 28 April. The 32 Class 254 HST sets were delivered between 1977 and 1979; HST operation of some of the principal trains on the East Coast Main Line had commenced with the 1978 summer timetable, and by the spring of 1979 some services between King's Cross and Leeds were also allocated to the new trains.

The diesel multiple unit (DMU) on the right also provides a good standard of accommodation for passengers; it is a Class 123 'Inter-City' unit built at BR Swindon Works in 1963. Originally used between Swansea, Birmingham and Derby, these units were transferred to Hull in 1977 to work on services across the Pennines. Gangwayed throughout, the carriages were very comfortable and the interior appointments matched the best locomotive-hauled stock of their day.

LEEDS The station seen in these photographs had been rebuilt in 1967 to become the single main station in Leeds. As part of that rebuild, services that had hitherto used nearby Leeds Central were rerouted into this completely remodelled station, which had previously been known as Leeds City. On the same day as the previous picture two Class 31 diesel-electric locomotives double-head a stone train past the station. The leading locomotive, No 31226, was to come to a premature end after an incident at Cricklewood during the early hours of Friday 28 October 1988; together with another locomotive, it rolled down a siding, crashed through the buffer stop and ended up partially blocking the A406 North Circular Road. The damage sustained proved terminal, and No 31226 was withdrawn at the end of December 1988. The second locomotive is No 31155, which remained in service until May 2000, a working life of more than 40 years.

Since these photographs were taken, Leeds station has again been extensively rebuilt between 1999 and 2002.

PENISTONE The LNER had started work on the electrification of the route from Manchester to Sheffield and Wath via Woodhead in 1938, but the project was soon halted by the outbreak of the Second World War. After work was resumed in 1946, it was found that the condition of the two single-bore tunnels at Woodhead was very poor, so they were replaced by a new Woodhead Tunnel, which took five years to complete and was formally opened by the Minister of Transport, Alan Lennox-Boyd, on 3 June 1954. Electric passenger services between Manchester and Sheffield commenced in September of that year. This route had always been noted for heavy freight traffic, and by the late 1960s it had been decided to concentrate all passenger traffic between Manchester and Sheffield on the more southerly Hope Valley route; passenger services via Woodhead were withdrawn in January 1970, allowing more paths for freight traffic. Ray Ruffell took this photograph of Penistone station on Thursday 17 May 1979 looking north-west. The electrified line to Manchester via Woodhead runs through the platforms on the left, while the line to Huddersfield, served by DMUs, curves away through the platforms on the right.

PENISTONE Substantial freight traffic was still carried by this route across Northern England in 1979, as illustrated by this Holyhead to Immingham working headed by two Class 76 Bo-Bo locomotives, Nos 76026 and 76021, photographed on the same day. Built for the electrification project, this batch of 58 rugged and reliable 1,500V DC locomotives gave splendid service on this route until 1981, although an obvious disadvantage on through workings was the need to change locomotives at each end of the electrified section.

Left: **PENISTONE** For many years the principal freight carried by the Woodhead route was coal from South Yorkshire to Fiddlers Ferry power station near Warrington. On Thursday 17 May Class 76 Bo-Bo locomotives Nos 76022 and 76029 approach Huddersfield Junction, immediately south of Penistone station, with a heavy 'merry-go-round' coal train for Fiddlers Ferry. The decline in the domestic coal industry and the establishment of major new power stations to supply the national grid, together with the fact that surplus capacity was now available on other east-west routes such as the Hope Valley line, meant that the writing was now on the wall for the Woodhead route, and it closed between Penistone and Hadfield in July 1981. Penistone station remains open and is served by Sheffield to Huddersfield diesel trains, but since May 1983 these have run via Barnsley rather than the old main line via Deepcar between Sheffield and Penistone.

Right: **ELLESMERE PORT** For many years the Manchester Ship Canal ran its own extensive standard-gauge railway system to facilitate the transfer of goods between ships and nearby industrial estates, notably the huge industrial estate at Trafford Park, and the national rail network. On Saturday 7 July 1979 the Wirral Railway Society enjoyed a tour of the MSC railway system, riding in open wagons hauled by Sentinel diesel locomotive No 3002. Note the ladder being used for access to the wagon next to the front brake-van. No 3002 was new in 1963, and was one of a number of diesels bought for the MSC system between 1959 and 1966. Sadly this network of lines went into decline in more recent years, and the last MSC trains ran in April 2009 at Trafford Park.

MARYPORT This station in Cumbria was originally the headquarters of the Maryport & Carlisle Railway, which operated the eponymous 28-mile line independently right up to the 1923 Grouping. There used to be an impressive office building and station here, including a clock tower, but sadly all was demolished in the 1970s and replaced by the simple shelter photographed by Ray Ruffell on Thursday 19 April 1979. From the opening of the station there has only ever been one long platform, signalled for use by trains in both directions – a very unusual feature on a double-track line. A two-car DMU provides ample accommodation for the 09.45 service from Carlisle to Lancaster.

In the autumn of 2011 a £120,000 refurbishment scheme, jointly funded by Northern Rail and Cumbria County Council, has seen the provision of new improved shelters and low-energy lighting at Maryport station.

1979 Happenings (1)

January
• Lorry drivers go on strike, causing shortages of some foods and, particularly, heating oil.
• Large numbers of other workers go on strike, causing serious disruption and giving rise to the title 'winter of discontent'.

February
• Many schools are forced to close owing to shortage of heating oil and/or strikes by ancillary staff.
• The TUC and the Government agree what becomes known as the 'St Valentine's Day Concordat', ending the 'winter of discontent'.
• St Lucia becomes independent of the United Kingdom.

March
• Penmanshiel Tunnel on the East Coast Main Line collapses (see next page).
• The Government loses a motion of confidence by one vote, and Prime Minister James Callaghan announces that a General Election will be held on 3 May.
• Airey Neave MP, Conservative Northern Ireland spokesman, is killed by an Irish National Liberation Army bomb in the House of Commons car park.
• The Royal Navy withdraws from Malta.

April
• Protester Blair Peach dies in London.

May
• The first section of London Underground's Jubilee Line opens.
• Margaret Thatcher becomes Prime Minister after the Conservative Party wins the General Election with a majority of 43.

June
• The first election for the European Parliament attracts a low turnout.
• Former Liberal Party leader Jeremy Thorpe is cleared of allegations of attempted murder.

PENMANSHIEL This location in southern Scotland, about 18 miles north-west of Berwick-on-Tweed, has featured in two very unusual events during the history of the East Coast Main Line between London and Edinburgh. On the evening of 23 June 1949 the 7.30pm Edinburgh to King's Cross train was approaching Penmanshiel Tunnel when fire broke out in the corridor of the tenth coach and spread with such incredible rapidity that two carriages of the 12-coach train were completely destroyed in a matter of minutes. The train was brought to an emergency stop partly inside the tunnel, and mercifully everyone on board escaped alive from this perilous situation. The rapid spread of the fire, which had probably been caused by discarded smoking materials, was the result of a highly inflammable varnish having been used in the construction of the carriages, which were two years old at the time of the incident.

Almost 30 years later, as part of a major scheme to permit the passage of larger containers on East Coast Main Line Freightliner trains, work was being carried out to increase the headroom in Penmanshiel Tunnel by lowering the tracks. At 03.45 on Saturday 17 March 1979 a sudden collapse of the tunnel roof deposited many tons of broken rock onto the railway. Thirteen of the men working in the tunnel at the time managed to get out, but sadly two men lost their lives, despite determined attempts to rescue them. One track through the tunnel had been kept in use while the work was carried out and it is indeed fortunate that no train was travelling along it at the time. In the aftermath of the tragedy it was soon apparent that it would be very difficult and expensive to remove the collapsed material and reopen the existing line. The tunnel was therefore abandoned and on 7 May 1979 work started on a new alignment in a cutting to the west of the former line. The rerouted track was opened to traffic on 20 August, and had therefore only been in use for a few days when Ray Ruffell took this photograph on the 23rd from the 14.15 Edinburgh to King's Cross train as it proceeded onto the new alignment.

1925. With longitudinal seating for 48 passengers, this car worked on routes across the Tyne to Newcastle and Gosforth as well as within Gateshead. Following the abandonment of the Gateshead tram system in 1951 car 10 passed to British Railways Eastern Region, which used it on the electrically operated Grimsby & Immingham Light Railway until that line closed in July 1961. Fortunately the car was saved for preservation and, restored to the former Gateshead livery, it continues in service at Beamish into the 21st century.

BEAMISH The North of England Open Air Museum at Beamish gives a wonderful taste of life as it was during the early years of the 20th century, using a variety of relocated and replica buildings together with a huge collection of working equipment and vehicles from the period. Transport is an important feature of the museum, and the site includes a tramway on which visitors can enjoy rides on a number of preserved cars. The weather was rather inclement when the Ruffell family visited on Saturday 13 October 1979, but Ray's wife Joan and daughter Margaret are clearly enjoying their ride on preserved single-deck tram No 10, which entered service at Gateshead in

CHESTER Nearest the camera in this line of DMUs awaiting their next turn of duty on Tuesday 15 May is Motor Brake 2nd No M50409, one of a small batch built by Park Royal Vehicles in 1957. Quite distinctive in appearance, the Park Royal units were particularly associated with services around Chester; note where the former headcode panel has been blanked off beneath the centre windscreen, and also the traditional oil tail lamp.

NORTHBOUND FROM EUSTON

1979 marked 100 years of refreshment cars on Britain's railway system – the first had operated in 1879 between Leeds and King's Cross on the Great Northern Railway. To mark the centenary, British Rail, Travellers

Fare and the National Railway Museum at York organised a special train made up of preserved refreshment cars from the Museum that ran tours over various parts of the network for a week.

Back in 1979 a good selection of normal British Rail service trains still carried restaurant cars, and having a relaxing meal during the journey was a very attractive feature of long-distance rail travel. This is well demonstrated by Ray's daughter Margaret as she makes a start on her breakfast while the 09.45 Euston to Lancaster proceeds northwards on Saturday 14 April. In a restaurant car the cornflakes would usually be followed by bacon, sausages, eggs, mushrooms, black pudding and fried bread, all silver-served, and the meal would conclude with toast and coffee – truly a great British breakfast. The subsequent reduction in the scale of on-board catering during the following 30 years is a change that has not met with universal customer approval.

Catch it while you can: the 'Marchwood Volunteer'

MARCHWOOD The Military Port at Marchwood, near Southampton, was established during the Second World War and includes a considerable complex of railway lines that are linked to the Totton to Fawley branch just south of the closed Marchwood station. On Saturday 21 July the Military Port and Railway held an open day, in connection with which the 'Marchwood Volunteer' rail tour ran from London Waterloo. A three-car DMU was provided, consisting of carriages built by the Pressed Steel Company in 1959, and it is seen at the Port Gate platform after arrival at the Military Port.

It was originally intended that after visiting Marchwood Military Port the rail tour would continue down the Fawley branch to Hythe to allow participants to walk through the town to visit Hythe Pier with its unique 2-foot-gauge railway (still operational in 2012, and now the oldest working electric pier railway in the world). Unfortunately it proved impossible to run the train onwards to Hythe on this occasion, so a later departure was made from Marchwood for Waterloo, and a chartered coach link was provided between Marchwood and Hythe for those who wanted to visit the pier railway.

The Totton to Fawley branch had opened in 1925 and by the mid-1960s the passenger service had been reduced to two trains each way on weekdays only, with timings to meet the needs of workers at Fawley refinery. It was therefore little surprise when passenger trains were withdrawn altogether in February 1966. Oil trains to Fawley and freight trains to and from Marchwood Military Port still run in 2012.

MARCHWOOD A most welcome presence at the open day was artist and conservationist David Shepherd. Known internationally for his paintings of wildlife, aircraft and the last days of steam on British Rail, David is actively involved in work to protect endangered species through the David Shepherd Wildlife Foundation.

David bought BR Standard 9F 2-10-0 No 92203 directly from British Rail after withdrawal in November 1967. The locomotive had been built at Swindon and entered service in April 1959, so was only used for a few years on the heavy freight work for which these locomotives were designed. After purchase by David Shepherd, No 92203 was moved under her own steam on the British Rail network from Crewe to the Longmoor Military Railway at Liss in Hampshire. It was there that the locomotive was named *Black Prince* – no name had been carried during No 92203's service with British Rail. When the Longmoor Military Railway was closed, *Black Prince* spent some time in store at Eastleigh before being moved to the East Somerset Railway at Cranmore.

At the Marchwood open day, David was photographed with some of his remarkable and atmospheric paintings, while *Black Prince* could be seen in partially restored condition. The locomotive was later to spend some time on the Gloucester & Warwickshire Railway, and at the time of writing is in service on the North Norfolk Railway at Sheringham.

BEDENHAM On the outward journey from Waterloo to Marchwood, the rail tour ran from Eastleigh via Botley to Fareham, then travelled down the remaining section of the Fareham to Gosport branch. This line had opened in 1841 and for many years played a vital role, especially carrying freight for the various victualling and armament yards in the area. In 1912 a link was opened from Bedenham to a network of lines serving the Naval depots at that location and at Priddy's Hard; an exchange siding (effectively a loop) was provided at Bedenham to allow for locomotives to be changed. Passenger services between Fareham and Gosport gradually dwindled in importance, and were withdrawn in June 1953. Freight services continued to run to Gosport until January 1969, after which only the section of line between Fareham and the MoD system at Bedenham RNAD was retained. It had originally been intended that the 21 July rail tour would travel onto the MoD railway system at Bedenham, but owing to an industrial dispute this proved impossible, so the train was reversed at the exchange siding, where travellers had the opportunity to alight and take photographs.

All rail operations ceased on the Fareham to Gosport branch in the 1990s, and on Sunday 22 April 2012 the section of the former trackbed between Redlands Lane and Tichborne Way was opened as the first phase of a dedicated busway, allowing services between Fareham and Gosport to avoid some of the heavy traffic on the parallel A32 road.

Winter tribulations on the Southern

GUILDFORD The Southern's third-rail electrified network is vulnerable in freezing weather, when ice can form on the top surface of the conductor rail. This severely reduces conductivity and results in arcing, which may cause serious electrical damage, including burnt-out shoe gear. One way of tackling the problem had been the operation of special de-icing trains. Some specific units were converted from elderly stock to perform this duty while running under their own power. In addition, four suburban trailer coaches, built in 1946 to augment pre-war units, were later converted to de-icing coaches and patrolled the network, normally sandwiched between two-car electric multiple units (EMUs). On Wednesday 24 January such a de-icing train has been formed using two 2-HAP units, but conditions are so severe that diesel-electric locomotive No 31414 has had to be called in to provide motive power for the train.

GUILDFORD Also called into use to assist stranded EMUs, 'Crompton' diesel-electric locomotive No 33206 is being detached from a 4-SUB unit at Guildford. In the right foreground 4-SUB unit No 4664, in service with BR from March 1950 until November 1980, awaits its next turn of duty.

GUILDFORD Everyone was working together to provide the best possible service in very challenging circumstances on 24 January. Here a motive power supervisor assists another supervisor who has been helping to chip ice from the buffers of 4-CIG unit No 7356 so that they could be extended to allow 'Crompton' diesel-electric locomotive No 33031 to be attached to the front of the train. The eight-car train was then hauled to Portsmouth by the Class 33, which had entered service in April 1961 as D6549 and was subsequently withdrawn in February 1989.

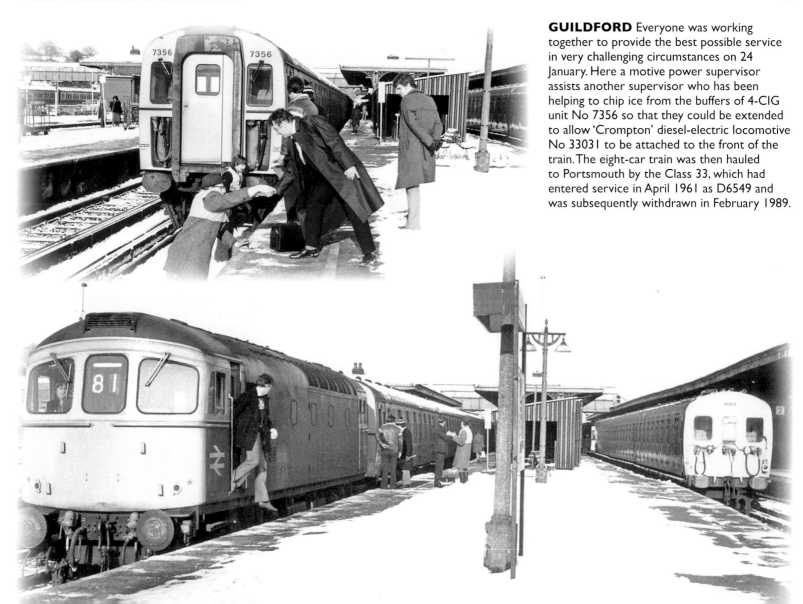

GUILDFORD This is the wintry scene looking towards London on Wednesday 24 January. A train of 4-SUB units is on the extreme left, while a 4-EPB unit has been berthed in the middle siding. An oil train for North Camp is about to depart behind a Class 37 diesel-electric locomotive while on the right an electro-diesel locomotive prepares to attach to a train formed of 4-VEP units, which will be hauled to Waterloo using diesel power only.

GUILDFORD This Portsmouth to London fast service, formed of 4-VEP and 4-CIG units, is being hauled by diesel-electric locomotive No 33011; new in June 1960 as No D6512, it was in service with BR until March 1989. The efforts by railway staff of all grades to maintain services in these conditions are deserving of the highest praise.

GUILDFORD The Class 73 electro-diesels were very useful and versatile locomotives, and certainly proved their worth in the severe conditions on 24 January. Here a member of the class, relying on its 600hp diesel generator, pushes the 4-CIG stock forming a Portsmouth to London fast service.

WATERLOO There does not necessarily have to be snow on the ground for ice on the conductor rails to cause problems. On Friday 26 January a service to Guildford via Ascot, formed of CIG stock, is having to be hauled by a diesel-electric locomotive owing to black ice on the conductor rails. Unusually, the train is departing from what was then Platform 15 at Waterloo; note the different roof line over the 1885-built section of the station on the left; the 1885 platforms were swept away in the early 1990s when the Eurostar station was built.

Catch it while you can: the 'Clydeside Wanderer'

ROTHESAY DOCK The 'Clydeside Wanderer' rail tour on Saturday 25 August departed from Glasgow Queen Street at 09.55 and ran to Glasgow Central, arriving at 18.50, along the way taking in a wealth of locations not normally visited by passenger trains. At 10.38 a 7-minute stop was made at Rothesay Dock, where the three-car Metropolitan-Cammell DMU is seen as the rail tour passengers explore this normally inaccessible location. The lines seen here were closed in 1983, but were used again in the 1990s for Rothesay Dock to Kincardine power station traffic, although this reinstatement was relatively short-lived and the railway is no longer in use here.

OLD KILPATRICK Legend has it that Old Kilpatrick, on the north bank of the River Clyde, was the birthplace of St Patrick. The rail tour made a 10-minute stop here; the Erskine Bridge can be seen in the background. This is the lowest point at which the River Clyde can be crossed by road and the impressive structure was opened by HRH Princess Anne on 2 July 1971.

Arrivals & Departures

Births

Rosamund Pike	Actress	27 January
Pete Doherty	Musician	12 March
Sophie Ellis-Bextor	Musician	10 April
Jonny Wilkinson	Rugby Union player	25 May
Jamie Harding	Actor	12 June
Allister Carter	Snooker player	25 July
Graeme McDowell	Golfer	30 July
David Healy	Footballer	5 August
Jamie Cullum	Musician	20 August
Stuart Fielden	Rugby League player	14 September
Stefan Booth	Actor	4 October
Aaron Hughes	Footballer	8 November
Simon Amstell	TV Presenter	29 November
Daniel Bedingfield	Musician	3 December
Michael Owen	Footballer	14 December

Deaths

Sid Vicious	Musician	(b1957)	2 February
Reginald Maudling	Politician	(b1917)	14 February
Richard Beckinsale	Actor	(b1947)	19 March
Airey Neave	Politician	(b1916)	30 March
Norman Hartnell	Fashion designer	(b1901)	8 June
Alfred Deller	Musician	(b1912)	16 July
Nicholas Monsarrat	Novelist	(b1910)	8 August
1st Earl Mountbatten of Burma		(b1900)	27 August
Gracie Fields	Musician	(b1898)	27 September
Rebecca Clarke	Musician	(b1886)	13 October
Barnes Wallis	Scientist	(b1887)	30 October
Merle Oberon	Actress	(b1911)	23 November
Joyce Grenfell	Actress	(b1910)	30 November

CLYDEPORT By late afternoon the rail tour had made its way to the south bank of the River Clyde, and proceeded from Paisley onto the branch to Clydeport at Greenock. Regular passenger trains on the branch to Princes Pier had ceased in 1959, although the line continued to be used by boat trains until 1965. The station at Princes Pier was demolished the following year, but the track was used by Freightliner trains until 1991. The rail tour followed the Clydeport branch as far as Union Street Tunnel, where a 10-minute stop was made. After everyone had reboarded, the train departed for Glasgow Central, via Paisley Gilmour Street.

Bristol fashion

BRISTOL TEMPLE MEADS Photographed on Friday 28 September, the magnificent main entrance building to Bristol Temple Meads station was designed by Sir Matthew Digby Wyatt and dates from 1878. The earliest parts of the buildings go back to 1840 and are out of sight to the left of this photograph. The station was further extended in 1935, and it is pleasing that this imposing building has been retained through later rationalisation and refurbishment works, and remains an impressive gateway to the railway network for the City of Bristol.

AVONSIDE WHARF A rather different view of Bristol Temple Meads station, in the background of this photograph taken on the same day, is that from Avonside Wharf. Note the enclosed bridge structure across the east end of the platforms, which was provided in the early 1970s for Post Office traffic. Avonside Wharf was the terminus of a line that had originally been constructed in the late 1820s to bring coal from Ram Pit colliery at Coalpit Heath into the centre of Bristol, initially using horses as motive power. In due course the line passed to the Midland Railway and by the mid-20th century was worked as a branch from Lawrence Hill to a Blue Circle Cement terminal at Avonside Wharf, which was still active in 1979. The last trains ran on this branch in the late 1980s and the site has now been built over as part of the Temple Quay redevelopment. Coal extraction from the Coalpit Heath area had ceased by the late 1940s when stocks were exhausted.

en route for Swansea. The utilitarian station buildings and footbridge were replaced in the early 21st century, and Bristol Parkway is now a popular and busy station.

On the same day the 10.23 Plymouth to Leeds train is formed of a mixture of BR Standard Mark 1 and Mark 2 stock and is hauled by Class 46 diesel-electric No 46030. Built at BR Derby works as D167 and entering service on 31 May 1962, this locomotive was renumbered 46030 in 1973 and remained in traffic until November 1981. Part of the spacious station car park can be seen on the right, with some vehicles that would now be regarded as classic cars.

BRISTOL PARKWAY This station was opened on 1 May 1972 and is located at Stoke Gifford on the line between Swindon and the Severn Tunnel. The new station was sited in an area with good road links and in easy reach of the motorway network, and this, together with the provision of ample parking facilities, was intended to attract car users to the trains. In addition, the population of this area to the north of Bristol was growing rapidly. The time is 15.32 on Friday 28 September 1979 and the 14.15 service from London Paddington, formed of HST unit No 253008, is calling at Bristol Parkway

WAPPING WHARF This location is not in London Docks, but on the south side of the Floating Harbour in Bristol. The Western Fuel Company operated this diesel locomotive, which was built by Hudswell Clarke & Company of Leeds in 1958. In 1979 Wapping Wharf was still linked to the British Rail network at Ashton Junction on the (by then) freight-only Portishead branch; on Thursday 6 December Ray was lucky enough to have a footplate trip as the locomotive returned from Ashton Junction to Wapping Wharf, where the staff were clearly pleased to be photographed with their locomotive. The Western Fuel Company continued to use Wapping Wharf for commercial coal traffic until 1987. Part of the site had been cleared by 2008, but plans for development were then put on hold owing to the economic situation. Nonetheless the area is still well worth a visit for the fascinating M-shed museum at nearby Princes Wharf, which tells the story of Bristol, while the preserved Bristol Harbour Railway, which runs on selected weekends, gives a taste of the atmosphere in days gone by.

Catch it while you can: the 'Night Ferry'

CLAPHAM JUNCTION While it operated, the 'Night Ferry' was a unique train on the British Rail network in that continental stock provided a through sleeping car service between London and Paris. The service had started on 14 October 1936, with the 1st Class sleeping cars being taken across the English Channel by train ferry between Dover and Dunkirk. On the outbreak of the Second World War in September 1939 the service was suspended, but resumed in December 1947. By the late 1970s the specially designed Wagons-Lits sleeping cars were more than 40 years old, and airlines had attracted most of the 1st Class clientele who had previously used this service. The stock for the 'Night Ferry' is seen travelling between Clapham Yard and London Victoria on Friday 4 May; note that most of the sleeping cars are in the traditional Wagons-Lits livery, although one has been given SNCF corporate identity. Note also the BR Standard Mark 1 Brake Corridor Composite coach bringing up the rear of the rake. When these photographs were taken the 'Night Ferry' had just under 18 months left to operate; the through sleeping car train departed from Victoria for the continent for the final time on the night of 31 October 1980. One of the unique Wagon-Lits sleeping cars has been preserved in the National Railway Museum at York. In the 21st century the Channel Tunnel provides regular through trains between London and the continent, but unfortunately proposals for through sleeping car trains did not come to fruition.

Welsh wanderings

CALDICOT One of the major railway masterpieces of Victorian engineering and building skills is the 4½-mile tunnel from Pilning to Caldicot beneath the River Severn. The Great Western Railway had obtained an Act of Parliament for the construction of the tunnel in 1872 and the first preparatory works began at Sudbrook Farm, Caldicot (near the location of these photographs), in March 1873. Construction was fraught with difficulty owing to water ingress and other problems, but the link was completed in 1885. In January 1886 a coal train from Aberdare to Southampton was the first to travel through the tunnel; regular freight trains commenced in September 1886, and passenger services followed three months later from 1 December. Altogether the tunnel had cost £1.8 million to build, but after opening the new route shortened journey times between Bristol and Cardiff by up to 90 minutes.

During the evening of Wednesday 6 June 1979 a three-car DMU forming a local service from Newport to Bristol heads away from the camera into the tunnel, while in the second view a Class 31 diesel locomotive with a short parcels working has just re-emerged into daylight and is heading for South Wales.

In 2012 the Severn Tunnel remains the principal rail route between London and South Wales; the huge outlay by the Great Western Railway in the 19th century has proved to have been a very sound investment.

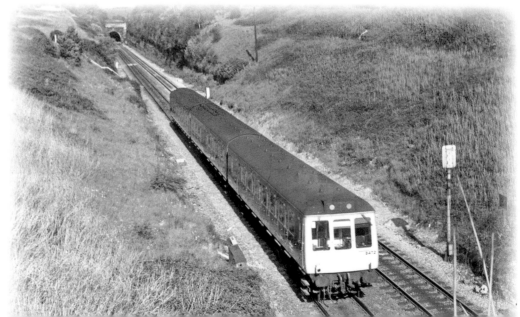

at that time never left the place in spirit, as there were a number of stories of a ghostly monk being seen around the steelworks. Of greater interest was the internal railway system, where the motive power included five imported locomotives that had been built by the American Locomotive Company (ALCO) in 1950. These 660hp diesels were numbered 801-805 while at work in South Wales, and Ray Ruffell photographed Nos 802 and 804 during a visit on Friday 12 January 1979. Subsequently No 802 was scrapped, but No 804 was preserved after withdrawal, and at the time of writing is located at Railworld, Peterborough.

PORT TALBOT Steelmaking in the Port Talbot area began with the Margam Iron & Steel works, built between 1923 and 1926. After the Second World War the Steel Company of Wales built the huge Abbey Steelworks between 1947 and 1951. The name was derived from the Cistercian Margam Abbey that had occupied this location prior to the dissolution of the monasteries by Henry VIII; it is possible that one of the residents displaced

Left: **PORT TALBOT** Also on Friday 12 January the 14.42 Swansea to London Paddington service, formed of HST unit No 253019, is seen arriving at Port Talbot. The station, which was opened in 1850, consists of a wide island platform linked by a footbridge to the ticket office in Talbot Road. After provision for car parking was increased in 1984, the station was renamed Port Talbot Parkway.

Below: **PORT TALBOT** 'Super-power' was needed to haul this 3,015-ton freight working from Port Talbot Ore Dock to Llanwern on Friday 6 April. No fewer than three Class 37 diesel locomotives, all based at Landore, Swansea, were provided for the working. Nos 37300, 37304 and 37308 had all entered service in 1965; No 37300 was withdrawn in 2002 and No 37304 in 1997, while No 37308 remained in service until 2005. Drivers V. Davies and W. G. Glass were photographed prior to leaving Port Talbot with their heavy train.

Below: **MISKIN** Notwithstanding the triple-headed super-power, the Port Talbot to Llanwern ore train has quite correctly been sidelined in the Miskin Loop to allow the HST unit forming the 15.43 Swansea to London Paddington service to overtake.

Right: **CYNHEIDRE** The colliery at Cynheidre was extensively developed by the National Coal Board from 1954 as a 'super pit', and the yard was full of loaded coal trucks when this photograph was taken on Friday 19 January 1979. The locomotive is No 37196, which entered traffic in 1964 as No D6896, was renumbered 37196 in 1973 and was to remain in service until September 2008. Despite the busy scene illustrated here, Cynheidre Colliery and the associated railway facilities closed in 1989. However, that was not the end of the story. The railway, which ran from Cross Hands to Llanelli via Cynheidre, had first opened as long ago as 1803 and was one of the first examples in Britain of freight being moved by rail. The Llanelli & Mynydd Mawr Railway Cynheidre Heritage Project aims to open a visitor centre incorporating a working railway and illustrating the heritage of the site; although at the time of writing no opening date had been fixed for this venture, fund-raising and work at the site by volunteers was ongoing and some items of rolling stock had been acquired.

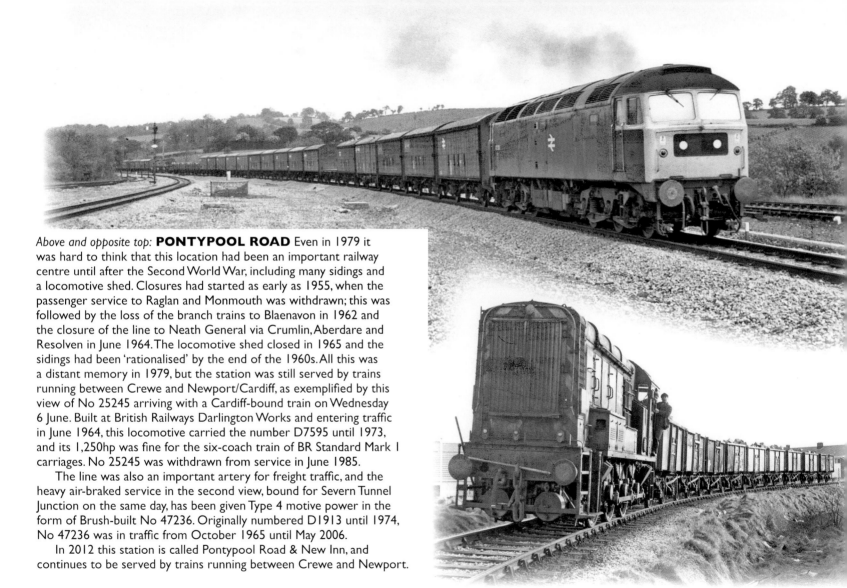

Above and opposite top: **PONTYPOOL ROAD** Even in 1979 it was hard to think that this location had been an important railway centre until after the Second World War, including many sidings and a locomotive shed. Closures had started as early as 1955, when the passenger service to Raglan and Monmouth was withdrawn; this was followed by the loss of the branch trains to Blaenavon in 1962 and the closure of the line to Neath General via Crumlin, Aberdare and Resolven in June 1964. The locomotive shed closed in 1965 and the sidings had been 'rationalised' by the end of the 1960s. All this was a distant memory in 1979, but the station was still served by trains running between Crewe and Newport/Cardiff, as exemplified by this view of No 25245 arriving with a Cardiff-bound train on Wednesday 6 June. Built at British Railways Darlington Works and entering traffic in June 1964, this locomotive carried the number D7595 until 1973, and its 1,250hp was fine for the six-coach train of BR Standard Mark 1 carriages. No 25245 was withdrawn from service in June 1985.

The line was also an important artery for freight traffic, and the heavy air-braked service in the second view, bound for Severn Tunnel Junction on the same day, has been given Type 4 motive power in the form of Brush-built No 47236. Originally numbered D1913 until 1974, No 47236 was in traffic from October 1965 until May 2006.

In 2012 this station is called Pontypool Road & New Inn, and continues to be served by trains running between Crewe and Newport.

Opposite bottom: **LLANELLI** With a total of 966 produced at various British Railways works between 1953 and 1962, the Class 08 diesel shunters were, in their day, numerically the most common locomotives on Britain's railway network. No 08660 entered traffic, numbered D3827, in May 1959 and was one of 153 of the class built at Horwich Works; it was renumbered 08660 in 1974. With 350hp at his disposal, driver Tom Heap had his train of nine loaded wagons nicely under control when photographed on the Llanelli Dock branch on Wednesday 7 March. No 08660 was withdrawn from service in November 1991.

Right: **USKMOUTH** As suggested by the name, Uskmouth power station is located at the mouth of the River Usk near Newport in south-east Wales. In 1979 the 'A' and 'B' power stations at this site were both coal-fired, and on Monday 11 June No 37247 has just delivered a trainload of coal. The happy crew are driver Bill Woodyatt standing in the cab doorway, secondman Ivor Holway looking through the window, and guard Dick Evans standing beside the locomotive. Built at the English Electric Vulcan Foundry and entering traffic as No D6947 in October 1964, this locomotive was renumbered 37247 in 1973, and subsequently became No 37671 in 1986. After withdrawal it was scrapped at Attercliffe (Sheffield) by European Metal Recycling in February 2011.

PENYFFORD Saturday 13 January was a bitterly cold day, and the 'Northwest Rambler' rail tour was disrupted when the severe weather caused delays in releasing the coaching stock from the sidings. Accordingly the tour train did not start from London Marylebone as planned, but a special DMU ran to connect with it at High Wycombe, from where it started to minimise the delay. By the time the tour reached Flintshire in the afternoon, the time had been made up, and participants took the opportunity to stretch their legs during a 15-minute stop. For this section of the journey Class 40 diesel-electric locomotive No 40108, in service with BR from November 1960 until August 1980, headed the train, which was formed of steam-heated BR Standard Mark 1 stock.

1979 Happenings (2)

July
- The 1,000th annual sitting of the Isle of Man Parliament, the Tynwald, takes place.
- Sebastian Coe sets a new record, running a mile in 3min 48.95sec.
- The Government announces £4 billion of public expenditure cuts.

August
- A strike by technicians causes the shutdown of the entire ITV network, which lasts until 23 October.
- A naturist beach is established in Brighton.
- The Fastnet yacht race is hit by storm in the Irish Sea, causing the loss of 15 lives.

- Lord Mountbatten of Burma is assassinated by a Provisional IRA bomb while on holiday in the Republic of Ireland.
- Eighteen British soldiers are killed in an ambush at Warrenpoint in Northern Ireland.

September
- Plans are announced for the regeneration of London's docklands with commercial and housing developments.
- An RAF Harrier jet crashes into a house in Wisbech, Cambridgeshire.
- Central Milton Keynes Shopping Centre is opened by Prime Minister Margaret Thatcher.

October
- All remaining foreign exchange controls are abolished.
- ITV television programmes return (see August).

November
- The Government announces a further £3.5 billion of public expenditure cuts.
- *The Times* newspaper resumes publication after a strike lasting almost a year.
- The minimum lending rate reaches 17%.
- Sir Anthony Blunt is revealed as a Soviet spy.

December
- The Housing Bill is published, giving council house tenants the right to buy their own homes from the following year.

HOLYHEAD The first station at Holyhead was opened by the Chester & Holyhead Railway in 1848; the structure with the overall roof, seen here on Tuesday 15 May 1979, was built by the London & North Western Railway in 1880. A DMU forming the 15.45 service to Llandudno awaits departure. A separate platform to the left of this photograph and close to the passenger ferry terminal building was used by most through trains to London, while the extensive Freightliner terminal can be seen on the right; the latter was commissioned in 1969, but the Britannia Bridge fire in 1970 effectively delayed opening to traffic until February 1971. The terminal was equipped with two Wellman Transport cranes for ship-to-shore movements, and two Goliath cranes for rail-to-road transfer. The growth of roll-on roll-off operations during the 1980s seriously reduced container traffic here, and Holyhead's Freightliner terminal was closed in the early 1990s, the site subsequently being used as a car park. It will be noted that bilingual running-in boards had been provided by 1979.

to the breakwater in 1967, delivering them by means of a road lorry. No D2954 had expired in 1971, but No D2955 (later renumbered 01002) survived until the line closed, supplemented from April 1975 onwards by Wickham motor trolley No TR23. This motor trolley was the only motive power operative on Tuesday 15 May 1979, but after being coupled to two four-wheel trolleys had no difficulty in hauling a new set of steel steps to the seaward end of the breakwater, where the steps were craned into the required position. By the summer of 1979 this unique line saw very little use and it was closed completely in 1980, with track-lifting starting in October of that year.

HOLYHEAD BREAKWATER

When he visited the Holyhead Breakwater Railway, Ray Ruffell described it as 'one of BR's strangest operations, being physically isolated from the rest of the system'. The line ran from Wild's Quarry to the seaward end of the Great Breakwater in Holyhead Bay and was mainly used to transport stone for the purposes of maintenance and repair to the breakwater. Responsibility for this had passed from the Board of Trade to the Ministry of Transport in 1934 and was transferred to the newly nationalised British Railways in 1948. BR allocated two diesel-mechanical shunters

Rocket 150

KENSINGTON GARDENS One of the best-documented events in the early history of railways in Britain is the Rainhill Trials, which took place in October 1829. It was a competition arranged by the directors of the Liverpool & Manchester Railway, with a prize of £500, then a very substantial sum of money, offered to the winning locomotive. As is well known, *Rocket*, designed by George and Robert Stephenson, won the trials, and the Stephensons were duly engaged to supply locomotives for the Liverpool & Manchester Railway. The L&MR could be described as the first double-track inter-city passenger-carrying railway in the world operating timetabled trains, and accordingly British Rail planned an event for 1980 to mark the 150th anniversary of this important antecedent. A re-enactment of the Rainhill Trials followed by a cavalcade of steam, diesel and electric locomotives, carriages and wagons, illustrating the development of railways over the 150-year period, took place on 24, 25 and 26 May 1980.

The replica of *Rocket* used for this event was built by Michael Satow and Locomotion Enterprises in 1979, and that summer it was operated on a special track laid in Kensington Gardens, London, to mark the 150th anniversary of the Rainhill Trials. These photographs were taken on Wednesday 29 August; the distinctive Albert Memorial can be seen in one of the views, while Michael Satow can be seen with a number of people watching the locomotive in steam in the other. The replica of *Rocket* is now in the care of the National Railway Museum, York, while the remains of the original locomotive that won the Rainhill Trials can be seen in the Science Museum, South Kensington, London.

A sojourn in Scotland

Above: **STIRLING** The Chipman weedkilling train is being hauled by Type 2 diesel-electric No 27005 on Thursday 28 June. Built by the Birmingham Railway Carriage & Wagon Company and entering service as No D5351 in 1961, this locomotive spent its working life allocated to Eastfield depot and was used on West Highland Line trains for a number of years. It is somewhat away from those haunts at Stirling, although the carriages in the weedkilling train are much further from their original home, having originated on the Southern Railway well before the Second World War. Remaining in service until July 1987, No 27005 was preserved by the Scottish Railway Preservation Society after withdrawal.

Right: **PITLOCHRY** After Queen Victoria's physician praised the healthy properties of the local air and climate, Pitlochry became something of a centre for visitors. The Highland Railway accordingly provided a station to complement the status of the town, with attractive stone offices on the up platform and equally pleasing wooden buildings on the down side. When photographed looking north on Thursday 16 August 1979, not a great deal had changed from 70 years previously; note the Highland Railway latticed iron footbridge.

However, the ornate cast-iron drinking fountain is not original to Pitlochry – it was transferred from Strathyre station after the closure of the line from Crianlarich to Callander in 1965. In the 21st century the Pitlochry Station Bookshop, staffed by volunteers with the cooperation and support of ScotRail, which allowed the use of previously unoccupied rooms in the station, has raised considerable sums for charities since opening in 2005.

Right: **LEUCHARS** On Tuesday 21 August, approaching Leuchars station, the 13.22 Dundee to Edinburgh service is formed of a three-car DMU; the leading car is in blue and grey livery with the other two in overall blue. The branch line on the right led to RAF Leuchars; this MoD line closed in the 1980s, although RAF Leuchars remains very much operational at the time of writing.

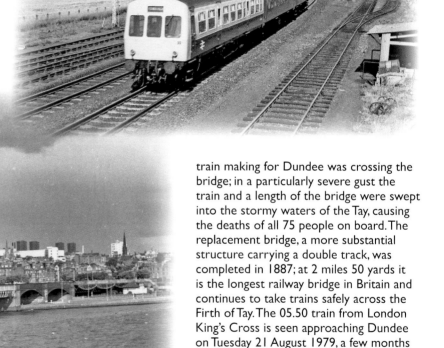

Below: **TAY BRIDGE** The first railway bridge across the Firth of Tay was opened to passenger traffic on 1 June 1878. It carried a single-track railway and unfortunately had not been designed or built to take into account the severe weather conditions experienced at this exposed location. On the evening of Sunday 28 December 1879 wind speeds were in excess of 80mph as a train making for Dundee was crossing the bridge; in a particularly severe gust the train and a length of the bridge were swept into the stormy waters of the Tay, causing the deaths of all 75 people on board. The replacement bridge, a more substantial structure carrying a double track, was completed in 1887; at 2 miles 50 yards it is the longest railway bridge in Britain and continues to take trains safely across the Firth of Tay. The 05.50 train from London King's Cross is seen approaching Dundee on Tuesday 21 August 1979, a few months short of 100 years since the disaster that befell the original Tay Bridge.

ARBROATH The station entrance building in Keptie Street can be seen on the overbridge in the background of this photograph; stairs lead down from the street-level booking hall to the platforms. The 12.40 train from Aberdeen was hauled by an unidentified Class 47 diesel-electric locomotive when photographed on Wednesday 15 August. The station buildings seen here were opened on Christmas Eve 1911 and replaced a station dating from 1848 on the same site. A centenary celebration for the present buildings was held in December 2011, which included music from the Arbroath Male Voice Choir.

TV favourites

Minder
The exploits of a used-car dealer, who also owned a lock-up from which he traded various items that had fallen off the backs of lorries, and his bodyguard made very enjoyable television. Arthur Daley (played by George Cole) and Terry McCann (Dennis Waterman) soon had the status of folk heroes; Arthur referred to his wife (never seen on screen) as ''er indoors', a term that soon passed into common usage.

Danger UXB
The dangerous and heroic life of a bomb disposal squad during the Second World War was brought to life in this series about these largely unsung heroes.

Shoestring
Trevor Eve played a computer boffin who, following a breakdown, offered a freelance problem-solving service for listeners who phoned in to a local radio station. Set in and around Bristol, the series was soon attracting high viewing figures.

Life on Earth
Sir David Attenborough's 13-part series about the advent of living species was rightly acclaimed as a masterpiece.

Question Time
Intended as a television version of Radio 4's *Any Questions?*, *Question Time* was first seen on our screens in 1979 and Sir Robin Day was the first presenter.

To the Manor Born
Set at Cricket St Thomas, Somerset, this popular comedy series starred Penelope Keith as Audrey Fforbes-Hamilton, a lady who had been forced by death duties to move to the lodge of her former stately home, which she had sold to businessman Richard de Vere (played by Peter Bowles).

Worzel Gummidge
Adapted by Keith Waterhouse and Willis Hall from the children's books by Barbara Euphan Todd and produced by Southern Television, this gentle series starred Jon Pertwee as the eponymous scarecrow and Una Stubbs as Aunt Sally, and was enjoyed by youngsters (and many adults).

Right: **MONTROSE** This location beside the Montrose Basin must have been a chilly spot when Ray photographed Class 25 diesel-electric No 25009 shunting the 07.00 freight from Dundee on Monday 5 February. Built at BR Darlington Works and entering service in July 1961 as No D5159, this locomotive was renumbered 25009 in 1973 and withdrawn in July 1980. A Class 40 passes with a passenger service of mostly BR Standard Mark 2 stock, but with a Mark 1 buffet car next to the locomotive. Montrose station, visible in the background, was later rebuilt by British Rail in 1983.

Left: **KINNABER JUNCTION** The Inter-City 125 HST unit forming the 09.00 service from Aberdeen to London King's Cross on Monday 5 February was photographed from a freight train on the Brechin line. HST units are still used for through services between Aberdeen and King's Cross in 2012, providing very comfortable accommodation for the journey of a little over 7 hours.

BRECHIN Passenger services to Brechin were withdrawn in August 1952, but a freight service was retained until May 1981, when the line between Brechin and Kinnaber Junction was closed entirely. These wintry scenes at the Brechin terminus were captured on Monday 5 February 1979; driver Ray Murphy has brought Class 25 locomotive No 25009 (seen earlier shunting at Montrose) with a freight service from Dundee on this bitterly cold morning. It will be seen that the station buildings are still largely complete despite passenger services having ceased more than 26 years before these photographs were taken. In 1979, with the future of the freight service looking doubtful, a preservation society was formed with the aim of restoring the line; this proved timely given the total closure two years later, as the 4-mile section between Brechin and Bridge of Dun has now been reopened as the heritage Caledonian Railway. The restoration of this terminus at Brechin is particularly worth seeing, as much of the original Victorian character has been retained.

INVERNESS A summer shower is in evidence as Class 40 diesel-electric No 40065 prepares to depart from Inverness with the 09.30 service to Edinburgh on Thursday 16 August. Built by English Electric at Vulcan Foundry and entering service in March 1960 as D265, this locomotive was renumbered 40065 in 1974. Based at Haymarket depot throughout its life, it was withdrawn in November 1981.

INVERNESS The marketing brand name 'Motorail' was first used by British Rail in 1966, although car-carrying services for motorists had been introduced some years previously. What in the 21st century would be regarded as classic cars have been secured on wagons ready for the journey south on the evening of Friday 17 August. Also of interest is the carriage on the extreme right of the photograph; it is a Griddle Car seating 12 passengers in a bar area (at the end further from the camera) and 18 in the buffet saloon at the other end. Note also the Mark 1 sleeping car to the left of the Motorail wagons.

The seating bay opposite the counter was also removed to provide a standing area. Such a carriage, Sc9276, was included in the 09.30 train from Inverness to Edinburgh on Thursday 23 August; note how the catering trolley fits neatly into the recess in the small counter. Stock security was excellent – all the attendant had to do was take the trolley when leaving the train.

INVERNESS The 'micro buffet' conversions were a clever way of providing a catering service on journeys where provision of a dedicated refreshment vehicle could not be justified. Some BR Standard Mark 1 Brake Open 2nds (BSOs) were modified by having a seating bay removed to make room for a small buffet counter into which would fit a standard on-train catering trolley, with facilities for making tea and coffee together with display space for other drinks, biscuits, sandwiches, etc.

ACHNASHEEN This interesting carriage was built by the Great Western Railway at Swindon in 1930. Numbered 9004, it was intended for the use of VIP parties and provided a high standard of accommodation with comfortable seating together with a small kitchen area so that if necessary the carriage could be a self-contained part of the train. Corridor connections were, however, provided, so that access to the rest of the train was available if desired. Windows were provided in the carriage ends and the end gangway doors, giving passengers panoramic views when the carriage was marshalled at the end of a train. On Monday 20 August 1979 this unique carriage had strayed far from its original stamping ground, forming part of the 10.30 service from Inverness to Kyle of Lochalsh; passengers are seen enjoying the extra comfort at Achnasheen.

KYLE OF LOCHALSH The exterior of coach No 9004 is seen by the buffer stop at the Kyle of Lochalsh terminus on the same day. Despite the time shown on the clock on the end of the station building, the carriage is at the rear of the 17.55 service to Inverness. The station at Kyle of Lochalsh enjoys a very scenic location on a wide stone pier, and the wooden station building, seen on the right, is in the centre of a broad island platform. Behind the photographer about half a mile of water separates the Isle of Skye from mainland Scotland.

AVIEMORE An unidentified Class 40 diesel-electric locomotive powers northwards with a train bound for Inverness on Wednesday 22 August. Situated amid the dramatic scenery of the Cairngorms National Park, Aviemore is a tourist destination of considerable importance, especially noted as a ski resort in winter. The line from Aviemore to Forres via Dava was closed to passengers in 1965, but the section between Aviemore and Boat of Garten was reopened by preservationists as the Strathspey Railway in 1978. The Strathspey Railway's trains were given access to the main-line station at Aviemore in 1998, and the reopened line was extended from Boat of Garten onwards to Broomhill in 2002. A trip on the line, especially on one of the superb evening dining trains, is highly recommended.

1979 No 1 records

January
YMCA	Village People
Hit Me With Your Rhythm Stick	Ian Dury & The Blockheads

February
Heart of Glass	Blondie

March
Tragedy	Bee Gees
I Will Survive	Gloria Gaynor

April
Bright Eyes	Art Garfunkel

May
Sunday Girl	Blondie

June
Ring My Bell	Anita Ward
Are 'Friends' Electric?	Tubeway Army

July
I Don't Like Mondays	Boomtown Rats

August
We Don't Talk Anymore	Cliff Richard

September
Cars	Gary Numan
Message in a Bottle	Police

October
Video Killed the Radio Star	Buggles
One Day at a Time	Lena Martell

November
When You're In Love With a Beautiful Woman	Dr Hook

December
Walking on the Moon	Police
Another Brick in the Wall	Pink Floyd

The Eling Tramway

ELING WHARF The Eling Tramway was a private siding that left the main London Waterloo to Weymouth line immediately west of Totton station; a sharp curve took the line to a level crossing over Totton High Street, then onwards to sidings near Southampton Water. For many years timber and tar were the principal merchandise being handled at Eling and, despite the general reduction in freight movements by rail at the time, the tramway was still handling a reasonable level of traffic during the 1960s. In 1973 Amalgamated Roadstone Corporation (ARC) opened a roadstone processing plant at Eling Wharf, which was connected to the tramway by a new siding used by trains bringing stone from Somerset. Class 47 diesel-electric locomotive No 47106 is seen at the stone depot with such a train on Monday 30 July 1979. Note the rail-mounted crane in the left distance. The sidings at the far end of the wharf among stacks of timber were also photographed on the same day.

Although a further new siding was added at Eling in 1987 to serve new warehouses for Redland Tiles, this proved to be the swansong for the Eling Tramway; workings for ARC ended in 1988 and the Redlands traffic ceased in 1990. The Eling Tramway was effectively closed when the points connecting it to the main line at Totton were removed in December 1993.

Catch it while you can: the 'Gwaun Cae Gurwen Growler'

Below: **ABERNANT** Rail tour participants take the opportunity to explore the sidings at Abernant Colliery, a location never served by passenger trains. The six-car train consists of (left to right) a Motor 2nd built by Birmingham RC&W, a Trailer Composite built by Pressed Steel, and a Motor Brake 2nd built by BRCW; all are of the suburban pattern with side doors to each seating bay, and carry overall blue livery. Next comes a three-car 'Cross Country' set, consisting of a Motor 2nd, a Trailer 2nd with miniature buffet section, and a Motor Brake Composite, all built at BR Swindon Works; these three coaches are painted in blue and grey livery, and contained much more comfortable accommodation than the three suburban carriages.

Above: **GWAUN CAE GURWEN** On Saturday 24 March the 'Gwaun Cae Gurwen Growler' rail tour explored a number of locations in South Wales, providing the opportunity to travel over lines not normally used by passenger trains at that time. Coal had always been the most important traffic handled at Gwaun Cae Gurwen, whose inhabitants only enjoyed a passenger service between 1908 and 1926. Out of sight to the left of this photograph is a four-arch brick viaduct built for a proposed line to carry coal to Clydach-on-Tawe and Swansea; the plans were deferred and the viaduct has never seen railway use.

Below: **ONLLWYN** Passenger services over the line from Neath to Brecon were withdrawn in October 1962, but the line between Neath and Onllwyn remains a busy freight route, mostly carrying coal traffic. On 24 March 1979 people are keen to look around the remains of the station and the still active colliery sidings. Passenger trains along the Neath and Brecon line had not been particularly frequent; for example, on weekdays during the late 1950s Onllwyn could boast a service of five trains per day to Neath and two per day (three on Saturdays) to Brecon. Onllwyn is now a coal distribution centre, processing the output from all of the sites operated by Celtic Energy.

Above: **PANTYFFYNNON** Fortunately passenger services still run on the very scenic Heart of Wales line from Swansea and Llanelli to Shrewsbury, operated at the time of writing by Arriva Trains Wales. It was on this line that the Gwaun Cae Gurwen rail tour encountered a flock of sheep that had decided to take a walk along the track, as photographed through the driver's windscreen by Ray Ruffell when the train was just south of Pantyffynnon.

In 2012 there are four trains per day each way on weekdays between Swansea and Shrewsbury; the journey of 121 miles takes around 4 hours, but a ride on this picturesque line is a delightful trip and greatly recommended.

Along London lines

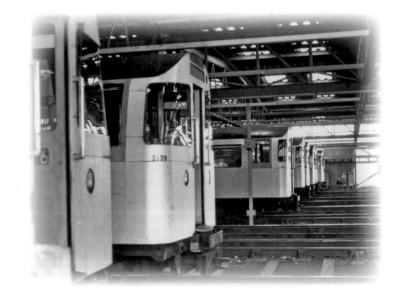

Below: **NORTHUMBERLAND PARK** Trains of London Transport 1967 tube stock await their next call to duty at Northumberland Park depot on Wednesday 29 August 1979. This stock operated the Victoria Line service for more than 40 years until replaced by the 2009 Stock between 2009 and 2011. Northumberland Park depot is the only point where the Victoria Line reaches the surface.

Above: **CUSTOM HOUSE** The railway reached North Woolwich in 1847, and to allow construction of the Victoria Dock a new alignment of the branch between Canning Town and Silvertown, including an intermediate station at Custom House, came into use in 1855. Until the Second World War passenger and freight traffic on the North Woolwich branch was heavy, but destruction of much of the area by bombing during that conflict, followed by altered travel patterns in the post-war period, had eroded the viability of the service by the early 1970s. However, the GLC provided funding for the reconstruction of some of the by then antiquated stations, and from 14 May 1979 a half-hourly service was provided between North Woolwich and Camden Road. On Friday 25 May a two-car DMU bound for North Woolwich enters Custom House station, where rebuilding work is under way. Subsequently the line was electrified in May 1985, with trains running through to Richmond. When the Docklands Light Railway was extended to Beckton in 1994 an adjacent station, also called Custom House, was opened on that line. The cessation of trains to North Woolwich in December 2006 brought about the closure of the platforms seen in this photograph; the DLR station remains and is the main public transport access for the ExCel Exhibition Centre.

Above: **WIMBLEDON** A very light dusting of snow was evident on Friday 5 January when Ray photographed Class 47 diesel-electric No 47072 on a stone train passing an eastbound R Stock District Line train. Entering service in 1965 as No D1656 and becoming 47072 under the TOPS scheme, this locomotive was again renumbered 47798 in March 1995, given the name *Prince William* and allocated to Royal Train duties. It was withdrawn in 2004 and is now preserved as part of the National Collection at York.

Car No 21146 at the rear of the District Line train to Tower Hill is also of interest. Entering service on 19 January 1953, it formed part of the first entirely unpainted aluminium train to run on the London Transport system, following earlier experiments with unpainted cars. It remained in service until October 1982, and the last R Stock trains ran on the District Line in March 1983.

Below: **WATERLOO** By 1979 Class 50 locomotives were coming into use on the Exeter to Waterloo line, replacing the lower-powered Class 33s that had provided the motive power from 1972 onwards. Numbered D433 when new in 1968 and first used on the West Coast Main Line between Crewe and Glasgow, No 50033 *Glorious* was photographed with the 06.15 service from Exeter on Monday 26 November 1979. This locomotive was preserved after withdrawal in 1994 and at the time of writing is at Tyseley. Class 50 operation continued on the Waterloo-Exeter line until the early 1990s; the service is now provided by Class 159 DMUs.

And so, like the 06.15 from Exeter, we arrive at the end of our journey. I hope you have enjoyed this look back at 1979.

Acknowledgements

It would not have been possible to produce this book without the use of the wonderful collection of photographs taken by the late Ray Ruffell; all of the illustrations in this volume started in his camera.

Ray was a railwayman by profession, but his interest in transport went far beyond his day-to-day work. In his off-duty time Ray travelled widely throughout the British Isles, and in doing so created an extensive photographic record of the railway system at a time when great changes were under way. Many scenes that were everyday and commonplace when Ray photographed them have now been swept away for ever and the memories he has captured on film, precious at the time, are now beyond price. It is pleasing to record that this huge collection of photographs has been kept complete and is now in the safe keeping of The NOSTALGIA Collection, forming an important part of the company's photographic archives.

I would like to say a sincere thank you to the team at The NOSTALGIA Collection for inviting me to write this book; the cheerful and willing help I have received from Peter Townsend, Will Adams and David Walshaw has been warmly appreciated and I feel deeply honoured to work with such kind people.

I hope you have enjoyed this book and will want to sample more years in the 'Railways & Recollections' series.

Index

HOLYHEAD BREAKWATER And so we end our nostalgic look back at 1979 with another glimpse of the unusual Holyhead Breakwater line. On Tuesday 15 May Ray Ruffell gives a broad grin to the camera as running repairs are carried out to Wickham trolley No TR23.